What is a Key Word?

A *Key Word* is a common word which your child [illegible] learn by sight. They are the building bricks of sentenc[illegible]se they appear so often. School reading schemes [illegible] *Key Words* so whatever scheme your child [illegible]e books will support it, they will reinfo[illegible]he learning and develop his/her rea[illegible]

Although *Key Words* are [illegible]sy to learn. Most children [illegible]e' than 'apple'. One of [illegible]y they can make a picture of [illegible]ake a mental picture for 'the'. Your chi[illegible]uragement.

What is an Incidental Word?

Other words, which are not *Key Words*, are introduced in the stories. This has been done to develop the second of the reading skills, that is, 'context'. The idea is that your child should try to guess the word by a) looking at the picture, b) thinking of a word which would make sense in the context of the sentence and story, and c) looking at the first letter of the word and thinking of a word that makes sense and starts with the right sound. Your child does not need to remember incidental words.

Attempting to read unknown words is very important. It is essential that you give your child lots of praise for a sensible guess. Never criticise an attempt, however wild. If the guess is wrong, supply the correct word, while praising the attempt.

Create a Feeling of Success

Your child must feel a sense of achievement for everything he/she reads. No matter how simple you think it is, give masses of praise. Young children need to feel that things are easy for them. If your child finds reading difficult, proceed very gently; find something which is easy so that he/she can develop a sense of success. Then you can pile on the praise and he/she will want to do more. Above all, don't push at this early stage. Keep it light-hearted and fun.

How to Use This Book

1. Write down the *Key Words* and show them to your child. Discuss the shape of the word, how many letters, what letter each starts with, etc. Write the words on separate cards and see if your child can learn one or two before starting the book. Find a page where a particular word appears and ask your child to point to the word.
2. If your child is quite confident, he/she might be happy to read straightaway. Otherwise, read the story aloud to your child first, pointing to each word as you do so. Spend time talking about the pictures because a great deal of the story is told in the pictures.
3. Ask questions, such as, 'What do you think will happen next?' Or 'Why did she do that?'
4. When your child starts to read the book, be very patient and encouraging. Never let him/her struggle over a word. Tell him/her what the word is.
5. Once you have reached the end of the book, encourage your child to read it as often as possible. One reading is not enough to learn the *Key Words*.
6. Use any of the activities suggested on page 28.
7. The text is specially designed to be read by a child who only knows the *Key Words* taught in this reading series. For this reason, you should start with the books in Level One and progress in order.
8. Avoid pressure and stress at all costs. Reading is fun.

Key Words introduced in this book:

We come in up tree but get down Don't Come The

Incidental Words:

friend Hello sand-pit stuck ladder worry

age 4-6

I can learn

Key Words readers

Come down, Silky!

Written by Nicola Morgan MA
an experienced teacher with a diploma in literacy teaching
Illustrations by Tina Freeman

Give lots of praise for reading, and stick the gold star reward sticker at the bottom of each right-hand page.

Key Words are printed in the coloured band at the foot of the page for the parent's reference.

Series editor: Nina Filipek
Series designer: Paul Dronsfield

Published in Great Britain in 1999 by
Egmont World Limited, Deanway Technology Centre,
Wilmslow Road, Handforth, Cheshire SK9 3FB.
Printed in Germany.
ISBN 0 7498 4100 1

Silky and Bouncy went to see
a friend.

Silky went up a tree.

I am stuck up in the tree,
said Silky.

I can go up but I can't
get down.

but get down

You can get down, said Dusty and Bouncy.

No, I can't, said Silky.

Dusty and Bouncy went to get a ladder.

You can get down the ladder,
said Bouncy.

Don't worry, said Dusty.

I can come up and you can come down, said Bouncy.

Don't worry, Silky.

Come on, Silky.
You can get down.

Come on. Come here.

Come down, Silky.

Silky is down, but oh no!

Now Bouncy is stuck in
the tree.

Don't worry, Bouncy.

The ladder is up.

Oh no! Look at Silky!

Silky is up the tree again!

Reading is not just identifying the words in a story. To be an effective reader, and to enjoy reading, your child needs to understand, appreciate and respond to a story in different ways.

Here are some useful activities for you to do with your child. The activities will help iron out any difficulties and will extend your child's enjoyment and appreciation of the story.

It is vital that all reading activities are fun, so do give plenty of praise; never push your child too much or work when he/she is tired, cross or hungry.

Reading skills: take all the key words introduced so far and make a bingo game. For each player, make a card divided into six sections, each with one of the key words written on it; make sure you also have each word written on a separate card and put these cards in a bag or box. In turn, each player takes a card; your child reads the word aloud; the player who has that word on his larger card shouts 'bingo' and places the word on the correct space on the card. The winner is the first player to fill all six spaces.

Writing: make a dictionary, with one page for each letter of the alphabet. Help your child write each word he/she knows on the correct page. Teach him/her how to find the word using alphabetical order skills. Add to it as your child learns new words.

Story-telling: tell a tall tale - take turns to say a few sentences of a story before handing over to the other person. Be as inventive as you wish! You could have an object which the story-teller holds and passes to the next person when it is that person's turn.

Following instructions: give your child instructions and see if he/she can follow them. Start off with simple ones, such as 'Go to the kitchen and bring me an apple'; then move to more complex ones, such as 'Go to the hall, put on your coat and boots, then come back here and sit on the floor'.

ONE TOKEN

Simply decide which gift you would like and collect the correct number of tokens. The more you collect the more money you can save.

	one token	two tokens	three tokens	four tokens	five tokens	
1 stationery case	£5.99	£5.49	£4.99	£4.49	£3.99	MAXIMUM 5 TOKENS
2 teaching clock	£5.99	£5.49	£4.99	£4.49	£3.99	MAXIMUM 5 TOKENS
3 calculator pencil case	£3.99	£3.49	£2.99	£2.49	£1.99	MAXIMUM 5 TOKENS
4 alphabet poster	£0.49	FREE				MAXIMUM 2 TOKENS
5 times tables poster	£0.49	FREE				MAXIMUM 2 TOKENS

Special Token

Please tape a £1 coin below to cover part post and packing costs.

£1

Please tick the offer you require above. You may also use the tokens available in other Egmont World books.

Please complete the following details:

I enclose a cheque made payable to Egmont World Limited for £______ (inc. p+p) Please send me the gift(s) I have indicated.

Name ________________________________

Age ________________________________

Address ________________________________

Postcode ________________________________

Title of this book purchased

Where it was purchased

Please return this completed form together with your tokens and a cheque or p.o. to:

Activity Centre Offers, Egmont World Limited, PO Box 7, Manchester M19 2HD.

Offer open to residents of UK, Channel Isles and Ireland only. Please allow 14 days for delivery. Egmont World Ltd. withholds the right to withdraw the offer. Offer subject to availability.

PLEASE STICK TOKENS BELOW

Place first token here	save 50p	save 50p	save 50p	save 50p

Once you have collected the required number of tokens, stick them to the spaces provided here and complete the form above.